TERCE, SEXT, NONE

according to the Benedictine ritual

LATIN - ENGLISH

Copyright © Clear Creek Abbey, 2021
All rights reserved.
ISBN: 978-1-329-97376-3

Clearcreekmonks.org

Contents

Sunday - Terce 3
Sunday - Sext 7
Sunday - None 11
Monday - Terce 15
Monday - Sext 21
Monday - None 27
Throughout the Week - Terce 33
Throughout the Week - Sext 40
Throughout the Week - None 47

SUNDAY — TERCE

℣. Deus in adjutórium meum inténde.
℟. Dómine ad adjuvándum me festína.   Glória Patri. –

℣. O God, come to my assistance.
℟. O Lord, make haste to help me.
Glory be to the Father.

Hymn

Nunc Sancte nobis Spíritus,
Unum Patri cum Fílio,
Dignáre promptus íngeri
Nostro refúsus péctori.

Os, lingua, mens, sensus, vigor,
Confessiónem pérsonent,
Flamméscat igne cáritas,
Accéndat ardor próximos.

Præsta, Pater piíssime,
Patríque compar Unice,
Cum Spíritu Paráclito
Regnans per omne sæculum.
        Amen.

Come, Holy Ghost, with God the Son
And God the Father ever One:
Shed forth Thy grace within our breast,
And dwell with us, a ready guest.

By every power, by heart and tongue,
By act and deed, Thy praise be sung:
Inflame with perfect love each sense,
That other's souls may kindle thence.

O Father, that we ask be done
Through Jesus Christ, Thine only Son,
Who, with the Holy Ghost and Thee,
Shall live and reign eternally.
        Amen.

Antiphon

In Advent, Septuagesima, Lent, and Passiontide, the Antiphon is as in the Proper of the Season.

In the Office of a Feast, the Antiphon is the second of those assigned to Lauds.

Throughout the year: **Allelúia † allelúia, allelúia.** (*in Paschaltide:* **Allelúia**)

Psalm 118

This psalm celebrates the joy of fidelity to God.

Legem pone mihi Dómine viam justificatiónum tuárum: * et exquíram eam semper.

Show me, O Lord, the way of Thy precepts, * and I will keep it to the end.

Da mihi intelléctum, et scrutábor legem tuam: * et custódiam illam in toto corde meo.

Deduc me in sémitam mandatórum tuórum: * quia ipsam vólui.

Inclína cor meum in testimónia tua: * et non in avarítiam.

Avérte óculos meos ne vídeant vanitátem: * in via tua vivífica me.

Státue servo tuo elóquium tuum, * in timóre tuo.

Amputa oppróbrium meum quod suspicátus sum: * quia judícia tua jucúnda.

Ecce concupívi mandáta tua: * in æquitáte tua vivífica me.

Glória Patri et Fílio *: et Spirítui Sancto.

Eᴛ veníat super me misericórdia tua Dómine: * salutáre tuum secúndum elóquium tuum.

Et respondébo exprobrántibus mihi verbum: * quia sperávi in sermónibus tuis.

Et ne áuferas de ore meo verbum veritátis usquequáque: * quia in judíciis tuis supersperávi.

Et custódiam legem tuam semper: * in sæculum et in sæculum sæculi.

Et ambulábam in latitúdine: * quia mandáta tua exquisívi.

Et loquébar in testimóniis tuis in conspéctu regum: * et non confundébar.

Give me intelligence to understand Thy law, * and I will observe it with all my heart.

Lead me on the path of Thy commandments, * for I delight therein.

Incline my heart unto Thy testimonies, * and not to covetousness.

Turn away mine eyes from beholding vanity, * enliven me upon Thy way.

Make good Thy promise to Thy servant, * and he will fear Thee.

Remove my reproach which I dread, * for excellent are Thy judgments.

Behold, I long for Thy statutes, * in Thy justice enliven me.

Glory be to Father and to the Son * and to the Holy Ghost.

Lᴇᴛ Thy mercy come upon me, Lord, * Thy salvation according to Thy promise.

Then shall I make answer to my slanderers, * for I trust in Thy word.

Do not utterly take from my mouth the word of truth, * for I rely upon Thy judgments.

Thy law will I keep unceasingly, * forever and ever.

So I shall walk at liberty, * for I seek Thy commandments.

Before kings will I speak of Thy testimonies, * and I shall not be confounded.

Et meditábar in mandátis tuis, * quæ diléxi.

Et levávi manus meas ad mandáta tua, quæ diléxi: * et exercébar in justificatiónibus tuis.

Memor esto verbi tui servo tuo, * in quo mihi spem dedísti.

Hæc me consoláta est in humilitáte mea: * quia elóquium tuum vivificávit me.

Supérbi iníque agébant usquequáque: * a lege autem tua non declínavi.

Memor fui judíciorum tuórum a sæculo Dómine: * et consolátus sum.

Deféctio ténuit me, * pro peccatóribus derelinquéntibus legem tuam.

Cantábiles mihi erant justificatiónes tuæ, * in loco peregrinatiónis meæ.

Memor fui nocte nóminis tui Dómine: * et custodívi legem tuam.

Hæc facta est mihi: * quia justificatiónes tuas exquisívi.–

I will meditate upon Thy precepts, * in which I take delight.

I lift my hands to Thy statutes which I love, * I will consider well Thy judgments.

Be mindful of Thy promise to Thy servant, * in which Thou gavest me to hope.

This is my solace in my distress, * that Thy word hath enlivened me.

The proud act wickedly without restraint, * but I do not swerve from Thy law.

I remember Thy judgments from of old, O Lord, * and find comfort in them.

My ire is roused against the sinners, * the forsakers of Thy law.

Like songs of joy are to me Thy statutes, * in the place of my pilgrimage.

I remember in the night Thy Name, O Lord, * and keep Thy precepts.

So is it with me, * that I observe Thy commandments.

Throughout the year:

Antiphon

Allelúia, allelúia, allelúia. (*in Paschaltide:* Allelúia)

Chapter — 1 John 4, 16

Deus cáritas est: et qui manet in caritáte, in Deo manet, et Deus in eo. ℟ Deo grátias.

God is love, and he who abides in love, abides in God, and God in him. ℟ Thanks be to God.

℣. Ego dixi: Dómine, miserére mei.
℟. Sana ánimam meam quia peccávi tibi.

℣. I say: O Lord, be merciful to me.
℟. Heal me, for I have sinned against Thee.

In other times of the year the Chapter is Proper.

Kyrie eléison. Christe eléison. Kyrie eléison.

Pater noster...
℣. Et ne nos indúcas in tentatiónem.
℟. Sed líbera nos a malo.
℣. Dóminus vobíscum.
℟. Et cum spíritu tuo.

Orémus.
Et dicitur oratio conveniens.
℣. Dóminus vobíscum.
℟. Et cum spíritu tuo.
℣. Benedicámus Dómino.
℟. Deo grátias.

Lord, have mercy on us. Christ, have mercy on us. Lord, have mercy on us.

Our Father, *silently until:*
℣. And lead us not into temptation.
℟. But deliver us from evil.
℣. The Lord be with you.
℟. And with your spirit.

Let us pray.
The proper Collect is said. Afterwards:
℣. The Lord be with you.
℟. And with your spirit.
℣. Let us bless the Lord.
℟. Thanks be to God.

SUNDAY — SEXT

℣. Deus in adjutórium meum inténde… | ℣. O God, come to my assistance…

Hymn

Rector potens, verax Deus,
Qui témperas rerum vices,
Splendóre mane ínstruis,
Et ígnibus merídiem.

Extíngue flammas lítium,
Aufer calórem nóxium,
Confer salútem córporum,
Verámque pacem córdium.

Præsta, Pater piíssime,
Patríque compar Unice,
Cum Spíritu Paráclito,
Regnans per omne sæculum.
Amen.

O God of truth, O Lord of might,
Disposing time and change aright,
Who clothes the splendid morning ray
And gives the heat at noon of day;

Extinguish Thou each sinful fire,
And banish every ill desire:
And while Thou keepest the body whole,
Shed forth Thy peace upon the soul.

O Father, that we ask be done
Through Jesus Christ, Thine only Son,
Who, with the Holy Ghost and Thee,
Shall live and reign eternally.
Amen.

Antiphon

In Advent, Septuagesima, Lent, and Passiontide, the Antiphon is as in the Proper of the Season.

In the Office of a Feast, the Antiphon is the third of those assigned to Lauds.

Throughout the year: **Allelúia † allelúia, allelúia.** (*in Paschaltide:* **Allelúia**)

Psalm 118

Pórtio mea Dómine, * dixi, custodíre legem tuam.
 Deprecátus sum fáciem tuam in toto corde meo: * miserére mei secúndum elóquium tuum.
 Cogitávi vias meas: * et

My portion it is, I say it O Lord, * to keep Thy law.
 I seek Thy face with all my heart; * have mercy on me according to Thy word.
 I think over my ways, * and turn my

convérti pedes meos in testimónia tua.
Parátus sum et non sum turbátus: * ut custódiam mandáta tua.
Funes peccatórum circumpléxi sunt me: * et legem tuam non sum oblítus.
Média nocte surgébam ad confiténdum tibi, * super judícia justificatiónis tuæ.
Párticeps ego sum ómnium timéntium te: * et custodiéntium mandáta tua.
Misericórdia tua Dómine plena est terra: * justificatiónes tuas doce me.

B ONITÁTEM fecísti cum servo tuo Dómine, * secundum verbum tuum.
Bonitátem, et disciplínam, et sciéntiam doce me: * quia mandátis tuis crédidi.
Priúsquam humiliárer ego delíqui: * proptérea elóquium tuum custodívi.
Bonus es tu: * et in bonitáte tua doce me justificatiónes tuas.
Multiplicáta est super me iníquitas superbórum: * ego autem in toto corde meo scrutábor mandáta tua.
Coagulátum est sicut lac cor eórum: * ego vero legem tuam meditátus sum.
Bonum mihi quia humiliásti me: * ut discam justificatiónes tuas.

feet unto Thy testimonies.
I stand prepared and unafraid * to observe Thy commands.
The snares of sinners have surrounded me, * but I do not forget Thy law.
In the middle of night I rise to praise Thee, * because of Thy righteous judgments.
I join in with all that fear Thee, * and that obey Thy precepts.
The earth, O Lord, is full of Thy mercy; * teach me Thy justifications.

T HOU hast dealt kindly with Thy servant, O Lord, * according to Thy word.
Teach me goodness and discipline and wisdom, * for I believe in Thy commandments.
Before I was humbled, I transgressed, * but now I heed Thy word.
Thou art good, * and in Thy goodness teach me Thy statutes.
The malice of proud men is heaped upon me, * but I will keep Thy law with all my heart.
Their heart is curdled like milk, * but I delight in Thy law.

It is good for me that Thou hast humbled me, * that I might learn Thy decrees.

Sunday - Sext

Bonum mihi lex oris tui, * super míllia auri et argénti.

Manus tuæ fecérunt me, et plasmavérunt me: * da mihi intelléctum, et discam mandáta tua.

Qui timent te vidébunt me, et lætabúntur: * quia in verba tua supersperávi.

Cognóvi Dómine quia æquitas judícia tua: * et in veritáte tua humiliásti me.

Fiat misericórdia tua ut consolétur me, * secúndum elóquium tuum servo tuo.

Véniant mihi miseratiónes tuæ, et vivam: * quia lex tua meditátio mea est.

Confundántur supérbi, quia injúste iniquitátem fecérunt in me: * ego autem exercébor in mandátis tuis.

Convertántur mihi timéntes te: * et qui novérunt testimónia tua.

Fiat cor meum immaculátum in justificatiónibus tuis, * ut non confúndar.

Dearer to me is the word of Thy mouth, * than gold and silver a thousandfold.

Thy hands have created me and fashioned me, * give me intelligence to understand Thy precepts.

Who fear Thee see me and rejoice, * because I rely upon Thy word.

I know, O Lord, that Thy judgments are just, * that in Thy fidelity Thou humblest me.

May Thy grace comfort me, * according to Thy promise to Thy servant.

Let Thy mercy come upon me that I may live, * for Thy law is my delight.

May the proud be shamed who oppress me unjustly, * but I meditate upon Thy commandments.

Let them side with me who fear Thee, * and who know Thy testimonies.

May my heart be blameless in Thy statutes, * that I may not be put to shame.

Throughout the year:
Antiphon
Allelúia, allelúia, allelúia. (*in Paschaltide:* Allelúia)

Chapter — Gal. 6, 2

Alter altérius ónera portáte, et sic adimplébitis legem Christi. ℟. Deo grátias.

Bear one another's burdens, and so you will fulfill the law of Christ. ℟. Thanks be to God.

℣. Dóminus regit me, et nihil mihi déerit.
℟. In loco páscuæ ibi me collocávit.

℣. The Lord is my shepherd and nothing is wanting to me.
℟. In green pastures He hath settled me.

In other times of the year the Chapter is Proper.

Kyrie eléison. Christe eléison. Kyrie eléison.

Lord, have mercy on us. Christ, have mercy on us. Lord, have mercy on us.

Pater noster...
℣. Et ne nos indúcas in tentatiónem.
℟. Sed líbera nos a malo.
℣. Dóminus vobíscum.
℟. Et cum spíritu tuo.

Our Father, *silently until:*
℣. And lead us not into temptation.
℟. But deliver us from evil.
℣. The Lord be with you.
℟. And with your spirit.

Orémus.
Et dicitur oratio conveniens.
℣. Dóminus vobíscum.
℟. Et cum spíritu tuo.
℣. Benedicámus Dómino.
℟. Deo grátias.
℣. Fidélium ánimæ, per misericórdiam Dei requiéscant in pace.
℟. Amen.
℣. Divínum auxílium máneat semper nobíscum.
℟. Et cum frátribus nostris abséntibus. Amen.

Let us pray.
The proper Collect is said. Afterwards:
℣. The Lord be with you.
℟. And with your spirit.
℣. Let us bless the Lord.
℟. Thanks be to God.
℣. May the souls of the faithful departed through the mercy of God rest in peace. ℟. Amen.
℣. May the divine assistance remain always with us.
℟. And with our absent brethren. Amen.

SUNDAY — NONE

℣. Deus in adjutórium meum inténde...

℣. O God, come to my assistance...

Hymn

Rerum, Deus, tenax vigor,
Immótus in te pérmanens,
Lucis diúrnæ témpora
Succéssibus detérminans:

Largíre clarum véspere,
Quo vita nusquam décidat,
Sed præmium mortis sacræ
Perénnis instet glória.

Præsta, Pater piíssime,
Patríque compar Unice,
Cum Spíritu Paráclito
Regnans per omne sæculum.
Amen.

O God, creation's secret force,
Thyself unmoved, all motion's source,
Who from the morn till evening's ray
Through all its changes guidest the day:

Grant us, when this short life is past,
The glorious evening that shall last;
That, by a holy death attained,
Eternal glory may be gained.

O Father, that we ask be done
Through Jesus Christ, Thine only Son,
Who, with the Holy Ghost and Thee,
Shall live and reign eternally.
Amen.

Antiphon

In Advent, Septuagesima, Lent, and Passiontide, the Antiphon is as in the Proper of the Season.

In the Office of a Feast, the Antiphon is the fifth of those assigned to Lauds.

Throughout the year: Allelúia † allelúia, allelúia. (*in Paschaltide:* Allelúia)

Psalm 118

Defécit in salutáre tuum ánima mea: * et in verbum tuum supersperávi.

Defecérunt óculi mei in elóquium tuum: * dicentes: Quando consoláberis me?

Quia factus sum sicut uter in pruína: * justificatiónes tuas non sum oblítus.

My soul doth pine for Thy salvation, * and I rely upon Thy word.

Mine eyes languish for Thy promise, * when wilt Thou comfort me?

I am become like a wineskin in the frost, * yet do I not forget Thy statutes.

Quot sunt dies servi tui? * quando fácies de persequéntibus me judícium?

Narravérunt mihi iníqui fabulatiónes: * sed non ut lex tua.

Omnia mandáta tua véritas: * iníque persecúti sunt me, ádjuva me.

Paulo minus consummavérunt me in terra: * ego autem non derelíqui mandáta tua.

Secúndum misericórdiam tuam vivífica me: * et custódiam testimónia oris tui.

IN ætérnum Dómine, * verbum tuum pérmanet in cælo.

In generatiónem et generatiónem véritas tua: * fundásti terram, et pérmanet.

Ordinatióne tua persevérat dies: * quóniam ómnia sérviunt tibi.

Nisi quod lex tua meditátio mea est: * tunc forte periíssem in humilitáte mea.

In ætérnum non oblivíscar justificatiónes tuas: * quia in ipsis vivificásti me.

Tuus sum ego, salvum me fac: * quóniam justificatiónes tuas exquisívi.

Me exspectavérunt peccatóres ut pérderent me: * testimónia tua intelléxi.

Omnis consummatiónis vidi finem: * latum mandátum tuum nimis.

How many still are the days of Thy servant? * when wilt Thou judge them that persecute me?

Idle tales have the wicked told me, * but nothing like to Thy law.

All Thy precepts are the truth; * the wicked pursue me, come Thou to help me.

They almost made an end of me on earth, * but I forsook not Thy commandments.

Enliven me according to Thy mercy, * that I may heed the counsels of Thy mouth.

FOR all eternity Thy word, O Lord, * standeth firm in heaven.

Thy truth endureth for all generations, * upon the earth which Thou hast created.

They endure till now according to Thy decree, * because all things must serve Thee.

Had not Thy law been my delight, * I should have perished in my misery.

Thy statutes shall I not forget forever, * for by them Thou hast enlivened me.

I am Thine, deliver me, * for I search out Thy judgments.

The wicked lie in wait for me to destroy me, * but I pay heed to Thy testimonies.

The limits I saw of all perfection; * broad, however, are Thy precepts.

Sunday - None

Quómodo diléxi legem tuam Dómine: * tota die meditátio mea est.

Super inimícos meos prudéntem me fecísti mandáto tuo: * quia in ætérnum mihi est.

Super omnes docéntes me intelléxi: * quia testimónia tua meditátio mea est.

Super senes intelléxi: * quia mandáta tua quæsívi.

Ab omni via mala prohíbui pedes meos: * ut custódiam verba tua.

A judíciis tuis non declinávi: * quia tu legem posuísti mihi.

Quam dúlcia fáucibus meis elóquia tua, * super mel ori meo.

A mandátis tuis intelléxi: * proptérea odívi omnem viam iniquitátis.

Oh, how I love Thy law, O Lord! * All the day it is my meditation.

By Thy precept Thou makest me wiser than my enemies, * for it is ever with me.

Better than all my teachers do I understand, * because I meditate upon Thy testimony.

More discernment have I than the elders, * because I keep Thy commandments.

From evil ways I keep my feet, * that I may heed Thy words.

From Thy judgments I do not turn aside, * because Thou gavest them as law to me.

How sweet to my palate are Thy promises, * sweeter than honey to my mouth!

Through Thy statutes I gain understanding; * therefore I hate every evil way.

Throughout the year:

Antiphon

Allelúia, allelúia, allelúia. (*in Paschaltide:* Allelúia)

Chapter — 1 Cor. 6, 20

Empti enim estis prétio magno. Glorificáte et portáte Deum in córpore vestro.

℟. Deo grátias.

℣. Ab occúltis meis munda me, Dómine.

℟. Et ab aliénis parce servo tuo.

For you have been bought at a great price. Glorify God and bear Him in your body.

℟. Thanks be to God.

℣. From my secret sins cleanse me, O Lord.

℟. And from strange evils spare Thy servant.

Sunday - None

In other times of the year the Chapter is Proper.

Kyrie eléison. Christe eléison. Kyrie eléison.	Lord, have mercy on us. Christ, have mercy on us. Lord, have mercy on us.
Pater noster...	Our Father, *silently until:*
℣. Et ne nos indúcas in tentatiónem.	℣. And lead us not into temptation.
℟. Sed líbera nos a malo.	℟. But deliver us from evil.
℣. Dóminus vobíscum.	℣. The Lord be with you.
℟. Et cum spíritu tuo.	℟. And with your spirit.
Orémus.	Let us pray.
Et dicitur oratio conveniens.	*The proper Collect is said. Afterwards:*
℣. Dóminus vobíscum.	℣. The Lord be with you.
℟. Et cum spíritu tuo.	℟. And with your spirit.
℣. Benedicámus Dómino.	℣. Let us bless the Lord.
℟. Deo grátias.	℟. Thanks be to God.
℣. Fidélium ánimæ, per misericórdiam Dei requiéscant in pace. ℟. Amen.	℣. May the souls of the faithful departed through the mercy of God rest in peace. ℟. Amen.
℣. Divínum auxílium máneat semper nobíscum.	℣. May the divine assistance remain always with us.
℟. Et cum frátribus nostris abséntibus. Amen.	℟. And with our absent brethren. Amen.

MONDAY — TERCE

℣. Deus in adjutórium meum inténde... | ℣. O God, come to my assistance...

Hymn

Nunc Sancte nobis Spíritus,
Unum Patri cum Fílio,
Dignáre promptus íngeri
Nostro refúsus péctori.

Os, lingua, mens, sensus, vigor,
Confessiónem pérsonent,
Flamméscat igne cáritas,
Accéndat ardor próximos.

Præsta, Pater piíssime,
Patríque compar Unice,
Cum Spíritu Paráclito
Regnans per omne sæculum.
Amen.

Come, Holy Ghost, with God the Son
And God the Father ever One:
Shed forth Thy grace within our breast,
And dwell with us, a ready guest.

By every power, by heart and tongue,
By act and deed, Thy praise be sung:
Inflame with perfect love each sense,
That other's souls may kindle thence.

O Father, that we ask be done
Through Jesus Christ, Thine only Son,
Who, with the Holy Ghost and Thee,
Shall live and reign eternally.
Amen.

In Ferial Office, throughout the year.

Antiphon

Adjúva me † et salvus ero Dómine. | Help me † and I shall be safe, O Lord.

In Advent time, Antiphon from Lauds of preceding Sunday or from proper Lauds.

In Lent:

Antiphon

Advenérunt nobis † dies pœniténtiæ, ad rediménda peccáta, ad salvándas ánimas. | Days of penance † are come to us, that we may redeem our sins and save our souls.

Monday - Terce

In Passiontide: (For Monday of Holy Week, proper Ant.).

Antiphon

| Judicásti Dómine † causam ánimæ meæ, defénsor vitæ meæ, Dómine Deus meus. | O Lord, † Thou hast pleaded the cause of my soul, O Lord my God, Thou defender of my life. |

In Paschaltide.

Antiphon

Allelúia, † allelúia, allelúia, allelúia.

In the Office of a Feast, the Antiphon is the second of those assigned to Lauds.

Psalm 118

Lucérna pédibus meis verbum tuum, * et lumen sémitis meis.	Thy word is a lamp unto my feet, * and a light for my path.
Jurávi, et státui * custodíre judícia justítiæ tuæ.	I swear and I am resolved * to obey Thy righteous judgments.
Humiliátus sum usquequáque Dómine: * vivífica me secúndum verbum tuum.	O Lord, I am bowed down exceedingly, * enliven me according to Thy promise.
Voluntária oris mei beneplácita fac Dómine: * et judícia tua doce me.	Take pleasure, O Lord, in the offerings of my mouth, * and teach me Thy precepts.
Anima mea in mánibus meis semper: * et legem tuam non sum oblítus.	My life is ever in my hands, * but I do not forget Thy law.
Posuérunt peccatóres láqueum mihi: * et de mandátis tuis non errávi.	The wicked are laying snares for me, * but I do not depart from Thy statutes.
Hæreditáte acquisívi testimónia tua in ætérnum: * quia exsultátio cordis mei sunt.	Thy testimonies I have chosen as my inheritance forever, * for they are the joy of my heart.
Inclinávi cor meum ad faciéndas justificatiónes tuas in ætérnum, * propter retributiónem.	I have set my heart on keeping Thy commandments, * because of thy reward forever.

Monday - Terce

Iníquos ódio hábui: * et legem tuam diléxi.
Adjútor et sucéptor meus es tu: * et in verbum tuum supersperávi.
Declináte a me malígni: et scrutábor mandáta Dei mei.
Súscipe me secúndum elóquium tuum, et vivam: * et non confúndas me ab exspectatióne mea.
Adjúva me, et salvus ero: * et meditábor in justificatiónibus tuis semper.
Sprevísti omnes discedéntes a judíciis tuis: * quia injústa cogitátio eórum.
Prævaricántes reputávi omnes peccatóres terræ: * ídeo diléxi testimónia tua.
Confíge timóre tuo carnes meas: * a judíciis enim tuis tímui.

Feci judícium et justítiam: * non tradas me calumniántibus me.

Súscipe servum tuum in bonum: * non calumniéntur me supérbi.
Oculi mei defecérunt in salutáre tuum: * et in elóquium justítiæ tuæ.
Fac cum servo tuo secúndum misericórdiam tuam: * et justificatiónes tuas doce me.

The wicked do I hate, * but Thy law is dear to me.
Thou art my helper and protector, * and I trust firmly in Thy word.
Depart from me, ye wicked ones, * and I will keep the commandments of my God.
Uphold me according to Thy word and I shall live, * and do not Thou fail me in my hope.
Help me and I shall be safe, * and I will ever take thought of Thy precepts.
Thou rejectest all who depart from Thy judgments, * because their thoughts are wicked.
All sinners of the earth I regard as liars; * therefore I love Thy testimonies.
Pierce Thou my flesh with the fear of Thee; * I stand in fear of Thy judgments.

I practise justice and righteousness, * abandon me not to my oppressors.
Receive Thy servant with favor, * let not the proud oppress me.
Mine eyes languish for Thy salvation, * and for Thy righteous promises.
Deal with Thy servant according to Thy mercy, * and teach me Thy statutes.

Servus tuus sum ego: * da mihi intelléctum, ut sciam testimónia tua.

Tempus faciéndi Dómine: * dissipavérunt legem tuam.

Ideo diléxi mandáta tua, * super aurum et topázion.

Proptérea ad ómnia mandáta tua dirigébar: * omnem viam iníquam ódio hábui.

I am Thy servant, * give me understanding, that I may know Thy testimonies.

It is time, O Lord, for action, * they have ignored Thy law.

Therefore do I love Thy precepts, * more than gold and precious stone.

Hence I am guided by all Thy commandments, * and I hate every evil path.

Throughout the year:

ANTIPHON

Adjúva me, et salvus ero Dómine.

Help me and I shall be safe, O Lord.

CHAPTER — *Jer. 17, 14*

SANA me, Dómine, et sanábor: salvum me fac, et salvus ero: quóniam laus mea tu es.

℣. Adjútor meus esto, ne derelínquas me.

℟. Neque despícias me, Deus, salutáris meus.

HEAL me, O Lord, and I shall be healed; save me and I shall be saved: for Thou art my praise.

℣. Be Thou my helper, forsake me not.

℟. Do not despise me, O God my Savior.

In Advent time, Antiphon from Lauds of preceding Sunday or from proper Lauds.

CHAPTER — *Jer. 23, 5*

ECCE dies véniunt, dicit Dóminus, et suscitábo David germen justum: et regnábit Rex, et sápiens erit: et fáciet judícium et justítiam in terra.

℟. Deo grátias.

℣. Veni ad liberándum nos, Dómine, Deus virtútum.

℟. Osténde fáciem tuam, et salvi érimus.

BEHOLD, the days come, saith the Lord, that I will raise unto David a righteous Branch; and a King shall reign and prosper, and shall execute judgment and justice in the earth. ℟. Thanks be to God.

℣. Come to save us, O Lord God of hosts.

℟. Show us the light of Thy countenance, and we shall be saved.

In Lent:

Antiphon

| Advenérunt nobis dies pœniténtiæ, ad rediménda peccáta, ad salvándas ánimas. | Days of penance are come to us, that we may redeem our sins and save our souls. |

Chapter — *Joel 2, 12-13*

| Convertímini ad me in toto corde vestro, in jejúnio, et fletu, et planctu. Et scíndite corda vestra, et non vestiménta vestra, ait Dóminus omnípotens.
℟. Deo grátias
℣. Ipse liberávit me de láqueo venántium.
℟. Et a verbo áspero. | Be converted to Me with all your heart, in fasting and in weeping and in mourning. And rend your hearts and not your garments, saith the Lord almighty.
℟. Thanks be to God.
℣. He hath delivered me from the snare of the hunters.
℟. And from the sharp word. |

In Passiontide (for Monday of Holy Week proper Ant.):

Antiphon

| Judicásti Dómine causam ánimæ meæ, defénsor vitæ meæ, Dómine Deus meus. | O Lord, Thou hast pleaded the cause of my soul, O Lord, my God, Thou defender of my life. |

Chapter — *Jer. 17, 13*

| Dómine, omnes qui te derelínquunt, confundéntur: recedéntes a te, in terra scribéntur: quóniam dereliquérunt venam aquárum vivéntium Dóminum.

℟. Deo grátias.
℣. Erue a frámea, Deus, ánimam meam.
℟. Et de manu canis únicam meam. | O Lord, all that forsake Thee shall be confounded; they that depart from Thee shall be written in the earth, because they have forsaken the Lord, the vein of living waters.
℟. Thanks be to God.
℣. Deliver my soul, O God, from the sword.
℟. And my only one from the power of the dog. |

Monday - Terce

In Paschaltide:

Antiphon

Allelúia, allelúia, allelúia, allelúia.

Chapter — Rom. 6, 9-10.

CHRISTUS resúrgens ex mórtuis jam non móritur, mors illi ultra non dominábitur. Quod enim mórtuus est peccáto, mórtuus est semel: quod autem, vivit, vivit Deo.
℟. Deo grátias.
℣. Surréxit Dóminus de sepúlchro, allelúia.
℟. Qui pro nobis pepéndit in ligno, allelúia.

FOR we know that Christ having risen from the dead, dies now no more, death shall no longer have dominion over Him. For the death that He died, He died to sin once for all, but the life that He lives, He lives unto God.
℟. Thanks be to God.
℣. The Lord has risen from the grave, alleluia.
℟. Who hung upon the Cross for us, alleluia.

For the Office of a Feast Day, proper Antiphon and Chapter.

Kyrie eléison. Christe eléison. Kyrie eléison.

Pater noster...
℣. Et ne nos indúcas in tentatiónem.
℟. Sed líbera nos a malo.
℣. Dóminus vobíscum.
℟. Et cum spíritu tuo.
℣. Orémus.
Et dicitur oratio conveniens.
℣. Dóminus vobíscum.
℟. Et cum spíritu tuo.
℣. Benedicámus Dómino.
℟. Deo grátias.

Lord, have mercy on us. Christ, have mercy on us. Lord, have mercy on us.

Our Father, *silently until:*
℣. And lead us not into temptation.
℟. But deliver us from evil.
℣. The Lord be with you.
℟. And with your spirit.
Let us pray.
The proper Collect is said. Afterwards:
℣. The Lord be with you.
℟. And with your spirit.
℣. Let us bless the Lord.
℟. Thanks be to God.

MONDAY — SEXT

℣. Deus in adjutórium meum inténde… | ℣. O God, come to my assistance…

Hymn

Rector potens, verax Deus,
Qui témperas rerum vices,
Splendóre mane ínstruis,
Et ígnibus merídiem.

Extíngue flammas lítium,
Aufer calórem nóxium,
Confer salútem córporum,
Verámque pacem córdium.

Præsta, Pater piíssime,
Patríque compar Unice,
Cum Spíritu Paráclito,
Regnans per omne sæculum.
Amen.

O God of truth, O Lord of might,
Disposing time and change aright,
Who clothes the splendid morning ray
And gives the heat at noon of day;

Extinguish Thou each sinful fire,
And banish every ill desire:
And while Thou keepest the body whole,
Shed forth Thy peace upon the soul.

O Father, that we ask be done
Through Jesus Christ, Thine only Son,
Who, with the Holy Ghost and Thee,
Shall live and reign eternally.
Amen.

In Ferial Office, throughout the year:

Antiphon

Adspice in me † et miserére mei Dómine. | Turn Thou to me † and show me mercy.

In Advent time, Antiphon from Lauds of preceding Sunday or from proper Lauds.
In Lent:

Antiphon

Commendémus nosmetípsos † in multa patiéntia, in jejúniis multis, per arma justítiæ. | With the armor of justice, † let us give ourselves to much patience and fasting.

In Passiontide (for Monday of Holy Week, proper Antiphon):

Antiphon

Pópule meus, † quid feci tibi? aut quid moléstus fui? Respónde mihi. | My people † what have I done to thee? Or in what have I grieved thee? Answer Me.

In Paschaltide:

Antiphon
Allelúia, † allelúia, allelúia, allelúia.

In the Office of a Feast, the Antiphon is the third of those assigned to Lauds.

Psalm 118

Mirabília testimónia tua: * ídeo scrutáta est ea ánima mea.

Declarátio sermónum tuórum illúminat: * et intelléctum dat párvulis.

Os meum apérui, et attráxi spíritum: * quia mandáta tua desiderábam.

Adspice in me, et miserére mei, * secúndum judícium diligéntium nomen tuum.

Gressus meos dírige secúndum elóquium tuum: * et non dominétur mei omnis injustítia.

Rédime me a calúmniis hóminum: * ut custódiam mandáta tua.

Fáciem tuam illúmina super servum tuum: * et doce me justificatiónes tuas.

Exitus aquárum deduxérunt óculi mei: * quia non custodiérunt legem tuam.

Justus es Dómine: * et rectum judícium tuum.

Mandásti justítiam testimónia tua: * et veritátem tuam nimis.

Tabéscere me fecit zelus meus: * quia oblíti sunt verba tua inimíci mei.

Wonderful are Thy testimonies, * hence my soul studieth them.

The doctrine of Thy word giveth light, * maketh wise the simple.

I open my mouth and draw breath, * for I long for Thy precepts.

Turn Thou to me and show me mercy, * according to Thy word to them that love Thee.

Establish my steps in Thy promises, * let no unrighteousness rule over me.

Deliver me from the oppression of men, * that I may keep Thy commandments.

Let Thy face shine upon Thy servant, * and teach me Thy statutes.

Streams of tears flow from mine eyes, * because they do not keep Thy law.

Thou art just, O Lord, * and upright is Thy judgment.

In righteousness hast Thou ordained Thy testimonies, * and in truth exceedingly.

My zeal consumeth me, * because my enemies are unmindful of Thy words.

Monday - Sext

Ignítum elóquium tuum veheménter: * et servus tuus diléxit illud.

Adolescéntulus sum ego et contémptus: * justificatiónes tuas non sum oblítus.

Justítia tua, justítia in ætérnum: * et lex tua véritas.

Tribulátio et angústia invenérunt me: * mandáta tua meditátio mea est.

Æquitas testimónia tua in ætérnum: * intelléctum da mihi, et vivam.

Clamávi in toto corde meo, exáudi me Dómine: * justificatiónes tuas requíram.

Clamávi ad te, salvum me fac: * ut custódiam mandáta tua.

Prævéni in maturitáte, et clamávi: * quia in verba tua supersperávi.

Prævenérunt óculi mei ad te dilúculo: * ut meditárer elóquia tua.

Vocem meam audi secúndum misericórdiam tuam Dómine: * et secúndum judícium tuum vivífica me.

Appropinquavérunt persequéntes me iniquitáti: * a lege autem tua longe facti sunt.

Prope es tu Dómine: * et omnes viæ tuæ véritas.

Inítio cognóvi de testimóniis tuis: * quia in ætérnum fundásti ea.

Thoroughly fire-tried is Thy word, * Thy servant taketh delight therein.

A youth am I and despised, * yet Thy judgments I do not forget.

Thy justice is justice eternally, * and Thy law is truth.

Trouble and anguish have befallen me, * yet are Thy precepts my delight.

Thy testimonies are forever just, * give me understanding that I may live.

With all my heart I cry, Lord, hear me, * I will observe Thy statutes.

I call upon Thee, save me, * I will obey Thy precepts.

In the early morning do I come and call, * for I trust in Thy word.

Mine eyes seek Thee before the early watch, * to meditate upon Thy promises.

Hear my voice, O Lord, in Thy mercy, * enliven me according to Thy judgment.

Pursuers of evil draw nigh to me, * but they are far from Thy law.

Thou, O Lord, art near to me, * and all Thy ways are truth.

Of old I knew of Thy testimonies, * that Thou hast founded them forever.

Throughout the year:

ANTIPHON

Adspice in me, et miserére mei Dómine. | Turn Thou to me and show me mercy.

CHAPTER — *Gal. 6, 2*

ALTER altérius ónera portáte, et sic adimplébitis legem Christi.

℣. Dóminus regit me, et nihil mihi déerit.

℟. In loco páscuæ ibi me collocávit.

BEAR one another's burdens, and so you will fulfill the law of Christ.

℣. The Lord is my shepherd and nothing is wanting to me.

℟. In green pastures He hath settled me.

In Advent time, Antiphon from Lauds of preceding Sunday or from proper Lauds.

CHAPTER — *Jer. 23, 6*

IN diébus illis salvábitur Juda, et Israel habitábit confidénter; et hoc est nomen quod vocábunt eum, Dóminus justus noster.

℟. Deo grátias.

℣. Osténde nobis, Domine, misericordiam tuam.

℟. Et salutáre tuum da nobis.

IN those days Juda shall be saved, and Israel shall dwell safely; and this is the Name whereby He shall be called, the Lord our Righteousness.

℟. Thanks be to God.

℣. Show us, O Lord, Thy mercy.

℟. And grant us Thy salvation.

In Lent:

ANTIPHON

Commendémus nosmetípsos in multa patiéntia, in jejúniis multis, per arma justítiæ. | With the armor of justice, let us give ourselves to much patience and fasting.

CHAPTER — *Isa. 55, 7*

DERELÍNQUAT ímpius viam suam, et vir iníquus cogitatiónes suas, et revertátur ad Dómi-

LET the wicked forsake his way, and the unjust man his thoughts; and let him return to the Lord and

num, et miserébitur ejus: et ad Deum nostrum, quóniam multus est ad ignoscéndum.
℣. Scápulis suis obumbrábit tibi.
℟. Et sub pennis ejus sperábis.

He will have mercy on him and to our God, for He is bountiful to forgive.
℣. With His pinions He will shelter thee.
℟. And under His wings thou shalt be secure.

In Passiontide (for Monday of Holy Week proper Antiphon):

ANTIPHON

Pópule meus, quid feci tibi? aut quid moléstus fui? Respónde mihi.

My people, what have I done to thee? Or in what have I grieved thee? Answer Me.

CHAPTER — *Jer. 17,18*

CONFUNDÁNTUR qui me persequúntur, et non confúndar ego: páveant illi, et non páveam ego: induc super eos diem afflictiónis, et dúplici contritióne cóntere eos, Dómine, Deus noster.
℟. Deo grátias.
℣. De ore leónis líbera me, Dómine.
℟. Et a córnibus unicórnium humilitátem meam.

LET them be confounded who persecute me, and let not me be confounded; let them be afraid, and let not me be afraid: bring upon them the day of affliction, and with a double destruction destroy them, O Lord our God.
℣. Save me from the lion's mouth, O Lord.
℟. And my lowliness from the horns of the unicorns.

In Paschaltide:

ANTIPHON

Allelúia, allelúia, allelúia, allelúia.

CHAPTER — *1 Cor. 15, 20-22*

CHRISTUS resurréxit a mórtuis, primítiæ dormiéntium: quóniam quidem per hóminem mors, et per hóminem resurréctio mor-

CHRIST has risen from the dead, the first fruits of those who have fallen asleep. For since by a man came death, by a Man also

tuórum. Et sicut in Adam omnes moriúntur, ita et in Christo omnes vivificabúntur.
℣. Surréxit Dóminus vere, allelúia.
℟. Et appáruit Simóni, allelúia.

comes resurrection of the dead. For as in Adam all die, so in Christ all will be made to live.
℣. The Lord is truly risen, alleluia.
℟. And hath appeared to Simon, alleluia.

For the Office of a Feast Day, proper Antiphon and Chapter.

Kyrie eléison. Christe eléison. Kyrie eléison.

Pater noster...
℣. Et ne nos indúcas in tentatiónem.
℟. Sed líbera nos a malo.
℣. Dóminus vobíscum.
℟. Et cum spíritu tuo.

Orémus.
Et dicitur oratio conveniens.
℣. Dóminus vobíscum.
℟. Et cum spíritu tuo.
℣. Benedicámus Dómino.
℟. Deo grátias.
℣. Fidélium ánimæ, per misericórdiam Dei requiéscant in pace.
℟. Amen.
℣. Divínum auxílium máneat semper nobíscum.
℟. Et cum frátribus nostris abséntibus. Amen.

Lord, have mercy on us. Christ, have mercy on us. Lord, have mercy on us.

Our Father, *silently until:*
℣. And lead us not into temptation.
℟. But deliver us from evil.
℣. The Lord be with you.
℟. And with your spirit.

Let us pray.
The proper Collect is said. Afterwards:
℣. The Lord be with you.
℟. And with your spirit.
℣. Let us bless the Lord.
℟. Thanks be to God.
℣. May the souls of the faithful departed through the mercy of God rest in peace. ℟. Amen.
℣. May the divine assistance remain always with us.
℟. And with our absent brethren. Amen.

MONDAY — NONE

℣. Deus in adjutórium meum inténde… | ℣. O God, come to my assistance.

Hymn

Rerum, Deus, tenax vigor,
Immótus in te pérmanens,
Lucis diúrnæ témpora
Succéssibus detérminans:

Largíre clarum véspere,
Quo vita nusquam décidat,
Sed præmium mortis sacræ
Perénnis instet glória.

Præsta, Pater piíssime,
Patríque compar Unice,
Cum Spíritu Paráclito
Regnans per omne sæculum.
Amen.

O God, creation's secret force,
Thyself unmoved, all motion's source,
Who from the morn till evening's ray
Through all its changes guidest the day:

Grant us, when this short life is past,
The glorious evening that shall last;
That, by a holy death attained,
Eternal glory may be gained.

O Father, that we ask be done
Through Jesus Christ, Thine only Son,
Who, with the Holy Ghost and Thee,
Shall live and reign eternally.
Amen.

In Ferial Office:, throughout the year:

Antiphon

Fiat † manus tua, Dómine ut salvum me fácias, quia mandáta tua concupívi. | Extend Thy hand, † O Lord, to save me, for I have chosen Thy commandments.

In Advent time, Antiphon from Lauds of preceding Sunday or from proper Lauds.

In Lent:

Antiphon

Per arma justítiæ † virtútis Dei commendémus nosmetípsos in multa patiéntia. | Let us prove ourselves † through much patience, in the armor of justice with the power of God.

In Passiontide (for Monday of Holy Week proper Antipon):

ANTIPHON

| Numquid rédditur † pro bono malum: quia fodérunt fóveam ánimæ meæ? | Shall evil † be rendered for good, because they have dug a pit for my soul? |

In Paschaltide:

ANTIPHON

Allelúia, † allelúia, allelúia, allelúia.

In the Office of a Feast, the Antiphon is the fifth of those assigned to Lauds.

PSALM 118

VIDE humilitátem meam, et éripe me: * quia legem tuam non sum oblítus.	LOOK upon my misery and deliver me, * for I do not forget Thy law.
Júdica judícium meum, et rédime me: * propter elóquium tuum vivífica me.	Plead my cause and redeem me, * enliven me according to Thy promises.
Longe a peccatóribus salus: * quia justificatiónes tuas non exquisiérunt.	Salvation is far from the wicked, * for they inquire not after Thy statutes.
Misericórdiæ tuæ multæ Dómine: * secúndum judícium tuum vivifíca me.	Great is Thy mercy, O Lord, * enliven me according to Thy judgment.
Multi qui persequúntur me, et tríbulant me: * a testimóniis tuis non declinávi.	Many are they that pursue and oppress me, * yet I do not swerve from Thy testimonies.
Vidi prævaricántes, et tabescébam: * quia elóquia tua non custodiérunt.	I see the evildoers and am grieved, * because they do not keep Thy precepts.
Vide quóniam mandáta tua diléxi Dómine: * in misericórdia tua vivífica me.	See, Lord, how I love Thy commandments, * enliven me according to Thy mercy.
Princípium verbórum tuórum, véritas: * in ætérnum ómnia judícia justítiæ tuæ.	The sum of Thy words is truth, * and Thy just judgements endure forever.

Monday - None

P RÍNCIPES persecúti sunt me gratis: * et a verbis tuis formidávit cor meum.
Lætábor ego super elóquia tua: * sicut qui invénit spólia multa.
Iniquitátem ódio hábui, et abominátus sum: * legem autem tuam diléxi.
Sépties in die laudem dixi tibi, * super judícia justítiæ tuæ.
Pax multa diligéntibus legem tuam: * et non est illis scándalum.
Exspectábam salutáre tuum Dómine: * et mandáta tua diléxi.
Custodívit ánima mea testimónia tua: * et diléxit ea veheménter.
Servávi mandáta tua et testimónia tua: * quia omnes viæ meæ in conspéctu tuo.

A PPROPÍNQUET deprecátio mea in conspéctu tuo Dómine: * juxta elóquium tuum da mihi intelléctum.
Intret postulátio mea in conspéctu tuo: * secúndum elóquium tuum éripe me.
Eructábunt lábia mea hymnum, * cum docúeris me justificatiónes tuas.
Pronuntiábit lingua mea elóquium tuum: * quia ómnia mandáta tua æquitas.
Fiat manus tua ut salvet me: * quóniam mandáta tua elégi.

T HE mighty oppress me without cause, * but my heart stands in fear of Thy word.
I rejoice over Thy promises, * as one who has found great booty.
I hate and abhor evildoing, * but I love Thy law.
Seven times a day do I praise Thee, * because of Thy righteous judgments.
Much peace have they that love Thy law; * for them there is no stumbling.
O Lord, I hope for Thy salvation, * and I love Thy commandments.
My soul keepeth Thy decrees, * and loveth them exceedingly,
I observe Thy precepts and Thy testimonies, * for all my ways are in Thy sight.

L ET my entreaty come before Thy face, O Lord, * grant me understanding according to Thy word.
Let my supplication come before Thee, * deliver me according to Thy promises.
My lips shall overflow with praise, * for Thou hast taught me Thy commands.
My tongue shall proclaim Thy word, * for all Thy laws are just.
Extend Thy hand to save me, * for I have chosen Thy commandments.

Concupívi salutáre tuum Dómine: * et lex tua meditátio mea est.
Vivet ánima mea, et laudábit te: * et judícia tua adjuvábunt me.
Errávi sicut ovis quæ périit: * quære servum tuum, quia mandáta tua non sum oblítus.

I yearn for Thy salvation, O Lord, * and Thy law is my delight.
May my soul live to praise Thee, * and may Thy judgments help me.
Like a sheep that is lost have I gone astray; * seek Thy servant, for I do not forget Thy laws.

Throughout the year:

Antiphon

Fiat manus tua, Dómine, ut salvum me fácias, quia mandáta tua concupívi.

Extend Thy hand O lord, to save me, for I have chosen Thy commandments.

Chapter — 1 Cor. 6, 20

Empti enim estis prétio magno. Glorificáte et portáte Deum in cópore vestro.
℟. Deo grátias.
℣. Ab occúltis meis munda me, Dómine.
℟. Et ab aliénis parce servo tuo.

For you have been bought at a great price. Glorify God and bear Him in your body.
℟. Thanks be to God.
℣. From my secret sins cleanse me, O Lord.
℟. And from strange evils spare Thy servant.

In Advent time, Antiphon from Lauds of preceding Sunday or from proper Lauds.

Chapter — Isa. 14, 1

Prope est ut véniat tempus ejus, et dies ejus non elongabúntur: miserébitur enim Dóminus Jacob et Israel salvábitur.
℟. Deo grátias.
℣. Super te, Jérusalem, oriétur Dóminus.
℟. Et glória ejus in te vidébitur.

Her time is near at hand, and her days shall not be prolonged. For the Lord will have mercy on Jacob, and Israel shall be saved.
℟. Thanks be to God.
℣. The Lord shall arise upon thee, O Jerusalem.
℟. And His glory shall be seen in thee.

Monday - None

In Lent:

Antiphon

Per arma justítiæ virtútis Dei commendémus nosmetípsos in multa patiéntia.

Let us prove ourselves through much patience, in the armor of justice with the power of God.

Chapter — Isa. 58, 7

Frange esuriénti panem tuum, et egénos vagósque induc in domum tuam: cum víderis nudum, óperi eum, et carnem tuam ne despéxeris.
℣. Scuto circúmdabit te véritas ejus.
℟. Non timébis a timóre noctúrno.

Deal thy bread to the hungry, and bring the needy and harborless into thy house; when thou shalt see one naked, cover him, and despise not thine own flesh.
℣. Like a shield His truth shall guard thee.
℟. Thou shalt not fear the terrors of night.

In Passiontide (for Monday of Holy Week proper Antiphon):

Antiphon

Numquid rédditur pro bono malum; quia fodérunt fóveam ánimæ meæ?

Shall evil be rendered for good, because they have dug a pit for my soul?

Chapter — Jer. 18, 20

Recordáre quod stéterim in conspéctu tuo ut lóquerer pro eis bonum, et avérterem indignatiónem tuam ab eis.
℟. Deo grátias.
℣. Ne perdas cum impiis, Deus, ánimam meam.
℟. Et cum viris sánguinum vitam meam.

Remember that I have stood in Thy sight to speak good for them, and to turn away Thy indignation from them.
℟. Thanks be to God.
℣. Destroy not my soul with the impious, O God.
℟. Nor my life with the men of blood.

Monday - None

In Paschaltide:

ANTIPHON

Allelúia, allelúia, allelúia, allelúia.

CHAPTER — *1 Peter 3, 18*

CHRISTUS semel pro peccátis nostris mórtuus est, justus pro injústis, ut nos offérret Deo, mortificátus quidem carne, vivificátus autem spíritu.
℣. Gavísi sunt discípuli, allelúia.
℟. Viso Dómino, allelúia.

BECAUSE Christ also died once for sins, the Just for the unjust, that He might bring us to God. Put to death indeed in the flesh, He was brought to life in the spirit.
℣. The disciples rejoiced, alleluia.
℟. At the sight of the Lord, alleluia.

For the Office of a Feast Day, proper Antiphon and Chapter.

Kyrie eléison. Christe eléison. Kyrie eléison.

Pater noster...
℣. Et ne nos indúcas in tentatiónem.
℟. Sed líbera nos a malo.
℣. Dóminus vobíscum.
℟. Et cum spíritu tuo.

Orémus.
Et dicitur oratio conveniens.
℣. Dóminus vobíscum.
℟. Et cum spíritu tuo.
℣. Benedicámus Dómino.
℟. Deo grátias.
℣. Fidélium ánimæ, per misericórdiam Dei requiéscant in pace.
℟. Amen.
℣. Divínum auxílium máneat semper nobíscum.
℟. Et cum frátribus nostris abséntibus. Amen.

Lord, have mercy on us. Christ, have mercy on us. Lord, have mercy on us.

Our Father, *silently until:*
℣. And lead us not into temptation.
℟. But deliver us from evil.
℣. The Lord be with you.
℟. And with your spirit.

Let us pray.
The proper Collect is said. Afterwards:
℣. The Lord be with you.
℟. And with your spirit.
℣. Let us bless the Lord.
℟. Thanks be to God.
℣. May the souls of the faithful departed through the mercy of God rest in peace. ℟. Amen.
℣. May the divine assistance remain always with us.
℟. And with our absent brethren. Amen.

THROUGHOUT THE WEEK
TERCE

℣. Deus in adjutórium meum inténde... | ℣. O God, come to my assistance...

Hymn

Nunc Sancte nobis Spíritus,
Unum Patri cum Filio,
Dignáre promptus íngeri
Nostro refúsus péctori.

Os, lingua, mens, sensus, vigor,
Confessiónem pérsonent,
Flamméscat igne cáritas,
Accéndat ardor próximos.

Præsta, Pater piíssime,
Patríque compar Unice,
Cum Spíritu Paráclito
Regnans per omne sæculum.
Amen.

Come, Holy Ghost, with God the Son
And God the Father ever One:
Shed forth Thy grace within our breast,
And dwell with us, a ready guest.

By every power, by heart and longue,
By act and deed, Thy praise be sung:
Inflame with perfect love each sense,
That other's souls may kindle thence.

O Father, that we ask be done
Through Jesus Christ, Thine only Son,
Who, with the Holy Ghost and Thee,
Shall live and reign eternally.
Amen.

On days commemorating the Blessed Virgin Mary, the doxology is changed to:

Glória tibi, Dómine, Qui natus es de Vírgine, Cum Patre et Sancto Spíritu, In sempitérna sæcula. Amen.

In Ferial Office throughout the year:

Antiphon

Clamávi † et exáudivit me. | I cry, † and He heareth me.

In Lent:
Antiphon

Advenérunt nobis † dies pœniténtiæ, ad rediménda peccáta, ad salvándas ánimas. | Days of penance † are come to us, that we may redeem our sins and save our souls.

In Passiontide (in Holy Week proper Antiphon):
Antiphon

Judicásti Dómine † causam ánimæ meæ, defénsor vitæ meæ, Dómine Deus meus. | O Lord, † Thou hast pleaded the cause of my soul, O Lord my God, Thou defender of my life.

In Paschaltide:
Antiphon

Allelúia, † allelúia, allelúia, allelúia.

In the Office of a Feast, the Antiphon is the second of those assigned to Lauds.

On Saturday commemorating Our Lady (except in Nativitytide):
Antiphon

Læva ejus † sub cápite meo, et déxtera ejus amplexábitur me (*T.P.* Allelúia). | His left hand † is under my head, and His right hand shall embrace me (*in Paschaltide:* Alleluia).

Psalm 119
The cry of a faithful in exile in the midst of deceptions.

Ad Dóminum cum tribulárer clamávi: * et exaudívit me.

Dómine líbera ánimam meam a lábiis iníquis, * et a lingua dolósa.

Quid detur tibi, aut quid apponátur tibi * ad linguam dolósam?

Sagíttæ poténtis acútæ, * cum carbónibus desolatóriis.

Heu mihi, quia incolátus meus prolongátus est: † habitávi cum habitántibus Cedar: * multum íncola fuit ánima mea.

To the Lord I cry in my distress * and He heareth me.

O Lord, deliver me from lying lips, * and from a deceitful tongue.

What shall be done to thee or meted out to thee, * thou treacherous tongue?

Sharp arrows be Thy portion, * together with coals of destruction.

Woe is me that I abide in Mesek, that I must dwell in Kedar's tents. * Too long already have I dwelt

Cum his qui odérunt pacem, eram pacíficus: * cum loquébar illis, impugnábant me gratis.

With them that hate peace. * I am peace-loving, but when I speak they war against me without cause.

Psalm 120

Confidence in the protecting tenderness of the Lord.

Levávi óculos meos in montes, * unde véniet auxílium mihi.

Auxílium meum a Dómino, * qui fecit cælum et terram.

Non det in commotiónem pedem tuum: * neque dormítet qui custódit te.

Ecce non dormitábit neque dórmiet, * qui custódit Israel.

Dóminus custódit te, Dóminus protéctio tua, * super manum déxteram tuam.

Per diem sol non uret te: * neque luna per noctem.

Dóminus custódit te ab omni malo: * custódiat ánimam tuam Dóminus.

Dóminus custódiat intróitum tuum et éxitum tuum: * ex hoc nunc, et usque in sæculum.

I lift up mine eyes to the mountains; * whence cometh help to me.

My help cometh from the Lord, * Who made heaven and earth.

He will not suffer thy foot to stumble, * He slumbereth not Who keepeth thee.

No, He slumbereth not, nor sleepeth * Who watcheth over Israel.

The Lord is thy protector and thy shelter, * the Lord is at thy right hand.

The sun shall not smite thee by day, * nor the moon by night.

The Lord keepeth thee from all evil, * the Lord protecteth thy life.

The Lord watched over thy coming and thy going, * from henceforth now and forever.

Psalm 121

Joy of the pilgrim arriving in Jerusalem.

Lætátus sum in his quæ dicta sunt mihi: * In domum Dómini íbimus.

Stantes erant pedes nostri, * in átriis tuis Jerúsalem.

Jerúsalem, quæ ædificátur ut cívitas: * cujus participátio ejus in idípsum.

I rejoiced when they said to me: * "Let us go into the house of the Lord"!

Already our feet are standing * at thy gates, O Jerusalem.

O Jerusalem, thou art built as a city * that is joined compactly together;

Illuc enim ascendérunt tribus, tribus Dómini: * testimónium Israel ad confiténdum nómini Dómini.

Quia illic sedérunt sedes in judício, * sedes super domum David.

Rogáte quæ ad pacem sunt Jerúsalem: * et abundántia diligéntibus te.

Fiat pax in virtúte tua: * et abundántia in túrribus tuis.

Propter fratres meos et próximos meos, * loquébar pacem de te:

Propter domum Dómini Dei nostri, * quæsívi bona tibi.

Throughout the year:

Whither the tribes go up, the tribes of the Lord; * it is a law for Israel, there to praise the name of the Lord.

For there stand the seats of judgment, * the seats of the house of David.

Pray now for peace upon Jerusalem: * "May they that love thee prosper!

Peace be within thy ramparts, * and repose within thy towers!

In behalf of my brothers and my friends * I bespeak thee peace.

In behalf of the house of the Lord our God, * I seek thee good".

Antiphon

Clamávi, et exáudivit me. | I cry, and He heareth me.

Chapter — Jer. 17, 14

Sana me, Dómine, et sanábor: salvum me fac, et salvus ero: quóniam laus mea tu es.

℟. Deo grátias.

℣. Adjútor meus esto, ne derelínquas me.

℟. Neque despícias me, Deus, salutáris meus.

Heal me, O Lord, and I shall be healed; save me and I shall be saved; for Thou art my praise.

℟. Thanks be to God.

℣. Be Thou my helper, forsake me not.

℟. Do not despise me, O God my Savior.

In Advent time from Lauds of preceding Sunday or from proper Lauds.

Chapter — Jer. 23, 5

Ecce dies véniunt, dicit Dóminus, et suscitábo David ger-

Behold, the days come, saith the Lord, that I will raise unto

men justum: et regnábit Rex, et sápiens erit: et fáciet judícium et justítiam in terra.
℟. Deo Grátias.
℣. Veni ad liberandum nos, Domine, Deus virtutum.
℟. Osténde faciem tuam, et salvi érimus.

David a righteous Branch; and a King shall reign and prosper and shall execute judgement and justice in the earth.
℣. Come to save us, O Lord God of hosts.
℟. Show us the light of Thy countenance, and we shall be saved.

In Lent:

ANTIPHON

Advenérunt nobis dies pœniténtiæ, ad rediménda peccáta, ad salvándas ánimas.

Days of penance are come to us, that we may redeem our sins and save our souls.

CHAPTER — *Joel 2, 12-13*

CONVERTÍMINI ad me in toto corde vestro, in jejúnio, et fletu, et planctu. Et scíndite corda vestra, et non vestiménta vestra, ait Dóminus omnípotens.
℟. Deo grátias.
℣. Ipse liberávit me de láqueo venántium.
℟. Et a verbo áspero.

BE converted to Me with all your heart, in fasting and in weeping and in mourning. And rend your hearts and not your garments, saith the Lord almighty.
℟. Thanks be to God.
℣. He hath delivered me from the snare of the hunters.
℟. And from the sharp word.

In Passiontide:

ANTIPHON

Judicásti Dómine causam ánimæ meæ, defénsor vitæ meæ, Dómine Deus meus.

O Lord, Thou hast pleaded the cause of my soul, O Lord my God, Thou defender of my life.

CHAPTER — *Jer. 17, 13*

DÓMINE, omnes qui te derelínquunt, confundéntur: recedéntes a te, in terra scribéntur:

O Lord, all that forsake Thee shall be confounded; they that depart from Thee shall be written in

quoniam dereliquérunt venam aquarum vivéntium Dóminum.
℟. Deo grátias.
℣. Erue a frámea, Deus, ánimam meam.
℟. Et de manu canis únicam meam.

the earth, because they have forsaken the Lord, the vein of living waters.
℟. Deo grátias.
℣. Deliver my soul, O God, from the sword.
℟. And my only one from the power of the dog.

In Paschaltide:

Antiphon

Allelúia, allelúia, allelúia, allelúia.

Chapter — Rom. 6, 9-10

CHRISTUS resúrgens ex mórtuis jam non móritur, mors illi ultra non dominábitur. Quod enim mórtuus est peccáto, mórtuus est semel: quod autem, vivit, vivit Deo.
℟. Deo grátias.
℣. Surréxit Dóminus de sepúlchro, allelúia.
℟. Qui pro nobis pepéndit in ligno, allelúia.

FOR we know that Christ having risen from the dead, dies now no more, death shall no longer have dominion over Him. For the death that He died, He died to sin once for all, but the life that He lives, He lives unto God.
℟. Deo grátias.
℣. The Lord has risen from the grave, alleluia.
℟. Who hung upon the Cross for us, alleluia.

For the Office of a Feast Day, proper Antiphon and Chapter.

On Saturday commemorating Our Lady (except in Nativitytide):

Antiphon

Læva ejus sub cápite meo, et déxtera ejus amplexábitur me (*T.P.* Allelúia).

His left hand is under my head, and His right hand shall embrace me (*in Paschaltide:* Alleluia).

Throughout the week - Terce

CHAPTER — *Ecclus. 24, 14*

AB inítio et ante sǽcula creáta sum, et usque ad futúrum sǽculum non désinam, et in habitatióne sancta coram ipso ministrávi.
℣. Spécie tua et puchritúdine tua.
℟. Inténde, próspere, procéde et regna.

FROM the beginning and before the world was I created, and unto the world to come I shall not cease to be, and in the holy dwelling place I have ministered before Him.
℣. In thy glory and thy splendor.
℟. Go forth, advance with victory and reign.

Kyrie eléison. Christe eléison. Kyrie eléison.

Pater noster...
℣. Et ne nos indúcas in tentatiónem.
℟. Sed líbera nos a malo.
℣. Dóminus vobíscum.
℟. Et cum spíritu tuo.

Orémus.
Et dicitur oratio conveniens.
℣. Dóminus vobíscum.
℟. Et cum spíritu tuo.
℣. Benedicámus Dómino.
℟. Deo grátias.

Lord, have mercy on us. Christ, have mercy on us. Lord, have mercy on us.

Our Father, *silently until:*
℣. And lead us not into temptation.
℟. But deliver us from evil.
℣. The Lord be with you.
℟. And with your spirit.

Let us pray.
The proper Collect is said. Afterwards:
℣. The Lord be with you.
℟. And with your spirit.
℣. Let us bless the Lord.
℟. Thanks be to God.

THROUGHOUT THE WEEK
SEXT

℣. Deus in adjutórium meum inténde... | ℣. O God, come to my assistance...

Hymn

Rector potens, verax Deus,
Qui témperas rerum vices,
Splendóre mane ínstruis,
Et ígnibus merídiem:

Extíngue flammas lítium,
Aufer calórem nóxium,
Confer salútem córporum,
Verámque pacem córdium.

Præsta, Pater piíssime,
Patríque compar Unice,
Cum Spíritu Paráclito,
Regnans per omne sæculum.
Amen.

O God of truth, O lord of might,
Disposing time and change aright,
Who clothes the splendid morning ray
And gives the heat at noon of day;

Extinguish Thou each sinful fire,
And banish every ill desire:
And while Thou keepest the body whole,
Shed forth Thy peace upon the soul.

O Father, that we ask be done
Through Jesus Christ, Thine only Son,
Who, with the Holy Ghost and Thee,
Shall live and reign eternally.
Amen.

On days commemorating the Blessed Virgin Mary, the doxology is changed to:
Glória tibi, Dómine, Qui natus es de Vírgine, Cum Patre et Sancto Spíritu, In sempitérna sæcula. Amen.

In Ferial Office: throughout the year:
Antiphon

Qui hábitas † in cælis miserére nobis. | Who art enthroned † in heaven, have mercy on us.

In Advent time, Antiphon from Lauds of preceding Sunday or from proper Lauds.

In Lent:

ANTIPHON

Commendémus nosmetípsos † in multa patiéntia, in jejúniis multis, per arma justítiæ.

With the armor of justice, † let us give ourselves to much patience and fasting.

In Passiontide:

ANTIPHON

Pópule meus, † quid feci tibi? aut quid moléstus fui? Respónde mihi.

My people, † what have I done to thee? Or in what have I grieved thee? Answer Me.

In Paschaltide:

ANTIPHON

Allelúia, † allelúia, allelúia, allelúia.

In the Office of a Feast, the Antiphon is the third of those assigned to Lauds.

On Saturday commemorating Our Lady (except in Nativitytide):

ANTIPHON

Nigra sum † sed formósa, fíliæ Jerúsalem: ídeo diléxit me rex, et introdúxit me in cubículum suum (T.P. Allelúia).

I am black, † but beautiful, O ye daughters of Jerusalem; therefore the King loved me, and brought me into His chamber (*Pasch.* Alleluia).

PSALM 122

The soul intent on Our Lord, praying for mercy.

Ad te levávi óculos meos, * qui hábitas in cælis.

Ecce sicut óculi servórum * in mánibus dominórum suórum.

Sicut óculi ancíllæ in mánibus dóminæ suæ: * ita óculi nostri ad Dóminum Deum nostrum donec misereátur nostri.

Miserére nostri Dómine, miserére nostri: * quia multum repléti sumus despectióne.

Unto Thee I lift up mine eyes, * Who art enthroned in heaven.

Behold, as the eyes of servants, * are upon the hand of their master,

As the eyes of the handmaid upon the hand of her mistress, * so are our eyes turned unto the Lord, until He showeth us mercy.

Have mercy on us, O Lord be gracious to us, * for we are overfilled with reproach.

Quia multum repléta est ánima nostra: * oppróbrium abundántibus, et despéctio supérbis.

We are overfilled with the taunts of the rich, * and with the contempt of the proud.

Psalm 123
Thanksgiving for a deliverance.

Nisi quia Dóminus erat in nobis, dicat nunc Israel: * nisi quia Dóminus erat in nobis.

Cum exsúrgerent hómines in nos, * forte vivos deglutíssent nos:

Cum irascerétur furor eórum in nos, * fórsitan aqua absorbuísset nos.

Torréntem pertransívit ánima nostra: * fórsitan pertransísset ánima nostra aquam intolerábilem.

Benedíctus Dóminus, * qui non dedit nos in captiónem déntibus eórum.

Anima nostra sicut passer erépta est * de láqueo venántium.

Láqueus contrítus est, * et nos liberáti sumus.

Adjutórium nostrum in nómine Dómini, * qui fecit cælum et terram.

If the Lord had not been with us, let Israel now say, * if the Lord had not been with us.

When men rose up against us, * they might have swallowed us alive.

When their fury was inflamed against us, * the waters might have rushed over us;

The torrent might have overwhelmed us, * the raging flood might have swept us along.

Blessed be the Lord Who hath not given us * as prey to their teeth.

Our soul hath escaped like a bird * out of the snare of the fowler.

The snare was broken through * and we are delivered.

Our help is in the Name of the Lord, * Who made heaven and earth.

Psalm 124
Security for him that lives in the Holy City, protected by God.

Qui confídunt in Dómino, sicut mons Sion: * non commovébitur in ætérnum, qui hábitat in Jerúsalem.

Montes in circúitu ejus: † et Dóminus in circúitu populí sui, * ex hoc nunc et usque in sæculum.

Those who trust in the Lord are like Mount Sion; * it shall not be moved forever, standing in Jerusalem.

As the mountains stand round about it, * so the Lord surroundeth His people now and forever.

Quia non relínquet Dóminus virgam peccatórum super sortem justórum: * ut non exténdant justi ad iniquitátem manus suas.

Bénefac Dómine bonis, * et rectis corde.

Declinántes autem in obligatiónes addúcet Dóminus cum operántibus iniquitátem: * pax super Israel.

The Lord will not let the sinners' rod weigh on the lot of the just, * lest the just extend their hands to evildoing.

Show Thy goodness, O Lord, to the good, * and to the upright of heart;

But strayers on crooked paths the Lord will snatch away like evildoers. * Peace upon Israel.

Throughout the year:

ANTIPHON

Qui hábitas in cælis miserére nobis.

Who art enthroned in heaven, have mercy on us.

CHAPTER — *Gal. 6, 2*

ALTER altérius ónera portáte, et sic adimplébitis legem Christi.

℣. Dóminus regit me, et nihil mihi déerit.

℟. In loco páscuæ ibi me collocávit.

BEAR one another's burdens, and so you will fulfill the law of Christ.

℣. The Lord is my shepherd and nothing is wanting to me.

℟. In green pastures He hath settled me.

Advent time from Lauds of preceding Sunday or from proper Lauds.

CHAPTER *Jer. 23, 6*

IN diébus illis salvábitur Juda, et Israel habitábit confidénter; et hoc est nomen quod vocábunt eum, Dóminus justus noster.

℟. Deo grátias.

℣. Osténde nobis, Domine, misericordiam tuam.

℟. Et salutáre tuum da nobis.

IN those days Juda shall be saved, and Israel shall dwell safely; and this is the Name whereby He shall be called, the Lord our Righteousness.

℣. Show us, O Lord, Thy mercy.

℟. And grant us Thy salvation.

In Lent:

ANTIPHON

Commendémus nosmetípsos in multa patiéntia, in jejúniis multis, per arma justítiæ.

With the armor of justice, let us give ourselves to much patience and fasting.

CHAPTER — *Isa. 55, 7*

Derelínquat ímpius viam suam, et vir iníquus cogitatiónes suas, et revertátur ad Dóminum, et miserébitur ejus: et ad Deum nostrum, quóniam multus est ad ignoscéndum.

℣. Scápulis suis obumbrábit tibi.

℟. Et sub pennis ejus sperábis.

Let the wicked forsake his way, and the unjust man his thoughts; and let him return to the Lord and He will have mercy on him and to our God, for He is bountiful to forgive.

℣. With His pinions He will shelter thee.

℟. And under His wings thou shalt be secure.

In Passiontide:

ANTIPHON

Pópule meus, quid feci tibi? aut quid moléstus fui? Respónde mihi.

My people, what have I done to thee? Or in what have I grieved thee? Answer Me.

CHAPTER — *Jer. 17, 18*

Confundántur qui me persequúntur, et non confúndar ego: páveant illi, et non páveam ego: induc super eos diem afflictiónis, et dúplici contritióne cóntere eos, Dómine, Deus noster.

℟. Deo grátias.

℣. De ore leónis líbera me, Dómine.

℟. Et a córnibus unicórnium humilitátem meam.

Let them be confounded who persecute me, and let not me be confounded; let them be afraid, and let not me be afraid: bring upon them the day of affliction, and with a double destruction destroy them, O Lord our God.

℣. Save me from the lion's mouth, O Lord.

℟. And my lowliness from the horns of the unicorns.

In Paschaltide:

Antiphon

Allelúia, allelúia, allelúia, allelúia.

Chapter — I Cor. 15, 20-22

CHRISTUS resurréxit a mórtuis, primítiæ dormiéntium: quóniam quidem per hóminem mors, et per hóminem resurréctio mortuórum. Et sicut in Adam omnes moriúntur, ita et in Christo omnes vivificabúntur.
℞. Deo grátias.
℣. Surréxit Dóminus vere, allelúia.
℞. Et appáruit Simóni, allelúia.

CHRIST has risen from the dead, the firstfruits of those who have fallen asleep. For since by a man came death, by a Man also comes resurrection of the dead. For as in Adam all die, so in Christ all will be made to live.
℞. Thanks be to God.
℣. The Lord is truly risen, alleluia.
℞. And hath appeared to Simon, alleluia.

For the Office of a Feast Day, proper Antiphon and Chapter.

On Saturday commemorating Our Lady (except in Nativitytide):

Antiphon

Nigra sum sed formósa, fíliæ Jerúsalem: ídeo diléxit me rex, et introdúxit me in cubículum suum (T.P. Allelúia).

I am black, but beautiful, O ye daughters of Jerusalem; therefore the King loved me, and brought me into His chamber (*Pasch.* Alleluia).

Chapter — Ecclus. 24, 15-16

ET sic in Sion firmáta sum, et in civitáte sanctificáta simíliter requiévi, et in Jerúsalem potéstas mea. Et radicávi in pópulo honorificáto, et in parte Dei mei hæréditas illíus, et in plenitúdine sanctórum deténtio mea.

℞. Deo grátias.

AND so was I established in Sion, and in the holy city likewise I rested, and my power was in Jerusalem. And I took root in an honorable people, and in the portion of my God His inheritance, and my abode is in the full assembly of Saints.

℞. Thanks be to God.

℣. Adjuvábit eam Deus vultu suo.
℟. Deus in médio ejus, non commovébitur.

Kyrie eléison. Christe eléison. Kyrie eléison.

Pater noster...
℣. Et ne nos indúcas in tentatiónem.
℟. Sed líbera nos a malo.
℣. Dóminus vobíscum.
℟. Et cum spíritu tuo.
Orémus.
Et dicitur oratio conveniens.
℣. Dóminus vobíscum.
℟. Et cum spíritu tuo.
℣. Benedicámus Dómino.
℟. Deo grátias.
℣. Fidélium ánimæ, per misericórdiam Dei requiéscant in pace.
℟. Amen.
℣. Divínum auxílium máneat semper nobíscum.
℟. Et cum frátribus nostris abséntibus. Amen.

℣. God shall help her with His countenance.
℟. God dwelleth in her, she shall not be moved.

Lord, have mercy on us. Christ, have mercy on us. Lord, have mercy on us.
Our Father, *silently until:*
℣. And lead us not into temptation.
℟. But deliver us from evil.
℣. The Lord be with you.
℟. And with your spirit.
Let us pray.
The proper Collect is said. Afterwards:
℣. The Lord be with you.
℟. And with your spirit.
℣. Let us bless the Lord.
℟. Thanks be to God.
℣. May the souls of the faithful departed through the mercy of God rest in peace. ℟. Amen.
℣. May the divine assistance remain always with us.
℟. And with our absent brethren. Amen.

THROUGHOUT THE WEEK
NONE

℣. Deus in adjutórium meum inténde… | ℣. O God, come to my assistance…

Hymn

Rerum, Deus, tenax vigor,
Immótus in te pérmanens,
Lucis diúrnæ témpora
Succéssibus detérminans:

  Largíre clarum véspere,
Quo vita nusquam décidat,
Sed præmium mortis sacræ
Perénnis instet glória.

  Præsta, Pater piíssime,
Patríque compar Unice,
Cum Spíritu Paráclito
Regnans per omne sæculum.
               Amen.

O God, creation's secret force,
Thyself unmoved, all motion's source,
Who from the morn till evening's ray
Through all its changes guidest the day:

  Grant us, when this short life is past,
The glorious evening that shall last;
That, by a holy death attained,
Eternal glory may be gained.

  O Father, that we ask be done
Through Jesus Christ, Thine only Son,
Who, with the Holy Ghost and Thee,
Shall live and reign eternally.
               Amen.

On days commemorating the Blessed Virgin Mary, the doxology is changed to:
Glória tibi, Dómine, Qui natus es de Vírgine, Cum Patre et Sancto Spíritu, In sempitérna sæcula. Amen.

In Ferial Office: throughout the year:

Antiphon

Beáti omnes † qui timent Dóminum. | Blessed are all, † who fear the Lord.

In Advent time Ant. from Lauds of preceding Sunday or from proper Lauds.

In Lent:

Antiphon

Per arma justítiæ † virtútis Dei commendémus nosmetípsos in multa patiéntia. | Let us prove ourselves † through much patience, in the armor of justice with the power of God.

In Passiontide:

ANTIPHON

| Numquid rédditur † pro bono malum; quia fodérunt fóveam ánimæ meæ? | Shall evil † be rendered for good, because they have dug a pit for my soul? |

In Paschaltide:

ANTIPHON

Allelúia, † allelúia, allelúia, allelúia.

For a saint's day, proper antiphon and Chapter or from the Common of Saints,

On Saturday commemorating Our Lady (except in Nativitytide):

ANTIPHON

| Speciósa facta es † et suávis in delíciis tuis, sancta Dei Génitrix (*T.P.* Allelúia). | Thou art beautiful † and sweet in thy delights, O holy Mother of God (*In Paschaltide:* Alleluia). |

PSALM 125

Return from the Captivity in Babylon.

IN converténdo Dóminus captivitátem Sion: * facti sumus sicut consoláti.

Tunc replétum est gáudio os nostrum: * et lingua nostra exsultatióne.

Tunc dicent inter gentes: * Magnificávit Dóminus fácere cum eis.

Magníficavit Dóminus fácere nobíscum: * facti sumus lætántes.

Convérte Dómine captivitátem nostram, * sicut torrens in Austro.

Qui séminant in lácrimis, * in exsultatióne metent.

Eúntes ibant et flebant, * mitténtes sémina sua.

WHEN the Lord ended the captivity of Sion, * we were then as in a dream.

Then our mouth was filled with gladness, * and our tongue with jubilation.

Then was it said among the heathens: * "The Lord hath done great things for them."

Yea, the Lord hath done great things for us; * and we were filled with joy.

Restore again, O Lord, our fortunes, * as the torrent in the south.

They who sow in tears * shall reap in gladness.

They go forth weeping, * sowing their seeds.

Veniéntes autem vénient cum exsultatióne, * portántes manípulos suos.

But they return rejoicing, * bearing their sheaves.

Psalm 126

Man depends entirely on God's help.

Nisi Dóminus ædificáverit domum, * in vanum laboravérunt qui ædíficant eam.

Nisi Dóminus custodíerit civitátem, * frustra vígilat qui custódit eam.

Vanum est vobis ante lucem súrgere: * súrgite postquam sedéritis, qui manducátis panem dolóris.

Cum déderit diléctis suis somnum: * ecce hæréditas Dómini, fílii: merces, fructus ventris.

Sicut sagíttæ in manu poténtis: * ita fílii excussórum.

Beátus vir qui implévit desidérium suum ex ipsis: * non confundétur cum loquétur inimicis suis in porta.

Unless the Lord build the house, * they labor in vain that build it;

Unless the Lord guard the City, * he watcheth in vain that guardeth it.

It is vain that you rise early, and late retire to rest, * ye who eat the bread of toil,

For to His loved ones He giveth it in sleep. * Behold, children are a gift from the Lord, the fruit of the womb a reward.

As arrows in the hand of a warrior, * so are the sons of vigorous youth.

Blessed is the man that hath his quiver filled with them: * he shall not be ashamed, when he speaketh with his enemies in the gate.

Psalm 127

Blessings granted by God to His faithful servants.

Beáti omnes, qui timent Dóminum, * qui ámbulant in viis ejus.

Labóres mánuum tuárum quia manducábis: * beátus es, et bene tibi erit.

Uxor tua sicut vitis abúndans, * in latéribus domus tuæ.

Blessed are all who fear the Lord, * who walk in His ways.

Thou shalt enjoy what thy hands earned: * blessed art thou, it shall be well with thee!

Thy wife is like a fruitful vine * on the walls of thy house;

Fílii tui sicut novéllæ olivárum, * in circúitu mensæ tuæ:
Ecce sic benedicétur homo, * qui timet Dóminum.
Benedícat tibi Dóminus ex Sion: * et vídeas bona Jerúsalem ómnibus diébus vitæ tuæ.
Et vídeas fílios filiórum tuórum. * Pacem super Israël.

Thy children like young olive trees, * round about thy board;
Behold, so shall the man be blessed, * who feareth the Lord.
Now the Lord bless thee from Sion; * and mayest thou see Jerusalem prosper all the days of thy life;
And mayest thou see thy children's children! * Peace upon Israel.

Throughout the year:

Antiphon

Beáti omnes qui timent Dóminum.

Blessed are all who fear the Lord.

Chapter — 1 Cor. 6, 20

EMPTI enim estis prétio magno. Glorificáte et portáte Deum in córpore vestro.
℣. Ab occúltis meis munda me, Dómine.
℟. Et ab aliénis parce servo tuo.

FOR you have been bought at a great price. Glorify God and bear Him in your body.
℣. From my secret sins cleanse me, O Lord.
℟. And from strange evils spare Thy servant.

Ant. Advent time from Lauds of preceding Sunday or from proper Lauds.

Chapter — Isa. 14, 1

PROPE est ut véniat tempus ejus, et dies ejus non elongabúntur: miserébitur enim Dóminus Jacob et Israel salvábitur.
℟. Deo grátias.
℣. Super te, Jérusalem, oriétur Dóminus.
℟. Et glória ejus in te vidébitur.

HER time is near at hand, and her days shall not be prolonged. For the Lord will have mercy on Jacob, and Israel shall be saved.
℟. Thanks be to God.
℣. The Lord shall arise upon thee, O Jerusalem.
℟. And His glory shall be seen in thee.

In Lent:

Antiphon

Per arma justítiæ virtútis Dei commendémus nosmetípsos in multa patiéntia.

Let us prove ourselves through much patience, in the armor of justice with the power of God.

Chapter — Isa. 58, 7.

Frange esuriénti panem tuum, et egénos vagósque induc in domum tuam: cum víderis nudum, óperi eum, et carnem tuam ne despéxeris.

℣. Scuto circúmdabit te véritas ejus.

℟. Non timébis a timóre noctúrno.

Deal thy bread to the hungry, and bring the needy and harborless into thy house; when thou shalt see one naked, cover him, and despise not thine own flesh.

℣. Like a shield His truth shall guard thee.

℟. Thou shalt not fear the terrors of night.

In Passiontide:

Antiphon

Numquid rédditur pro bono malum; quia fodérunt fóveam ánimæ meæ?

Shall evil be rendered for good, because they have dug a pit for my soul?

Chapter — Jer. 18, 20.

Recordáre quod stéterim in conspéctu tuo ut lóquerer pro eis bonum, et avérterem indignatiónem tuam ab eis.

℣. Ne perdas cum impiis, Deus, ánimam meam.

℟. Et cum viris sánguinum vitam meam.

Remember that I have stood in Thy sight to speak good for them, and to turn away Thy indignation from them.

℣. Destroy not my soul with the impious, O God.

℟. Nor my life with the men of blood.

In Paschaltide:

Antiphon

Allelúia, allelúia, allelúia, allelúia.

Chapter — 1 Pet. 3, 18

Christus semel pro peccátis nostris mórtuus est, justus pro injústis, ut nos offérret Deo, mortificatus quidem carne, vivificátus autem spiritu.
℣. Gavísi sunt discípuli, allelúia.
℟. Viso Dómino, allelúia.

Because Christ also died once for sins, the Just for the unjust, that He might bring us to God. Put to death indeed in the flesh, He was brought to life in the spirit.
℣. The disciples rejoiced, alleluia.
℟. At the sight of the Lord, alleluia.

For the Office of a Feast Day, proper Antiphon and Chapter.

On Saturday commemorating Our Lady (except in Nativitytide):

Antiphon

Speciósa facta es et suávis in delíciis tuis, sancta Dei Génitrix (*T.P.* Allelúia).

Thou art beautiful and sweet in thy delights, O holy Mother of God (*In Paschaltide:* Alleluia).

Chapter — Ecclus. 24, 19-20

In platéis, sicut cinnamómum et bálsamum aromatízans odórem dedi: quasi myrrha elécta, dedi suavitátem odóris.
℣. Elégit eam Deus, et præelégit eam.
℟. In tabernáculo suo habitáre facit eam.

In the plains I gave a sweet smell like cinnamon and aromatical balm: I yielded a sweet odor like the best myrrh.
℣. God hath selected her and hath chosen her.
℟. He hath made her dwell in His tabernacle.

Kyrie eléison. Christe eléison. Kyrie eléison.

Lord, have mercy on us. Christ, have mercy on us. Lord, have mercy on us.

Pater noster...
℣. Et ne nos indúcas in tentatiónem.
℟. Sed líbera nos a malo.
℣. Dóminus vobíscum.
℟. Et cum spíritu tuo.
Et dicitur oratio conveniens.

Our Father, *silently until:*
℣. And lead us not into temptation.
℟. But deliver us from evil.
℣. The Lord be with you.
℟. And with your spirit.
Collect. Let us pray.

Angelus

℣. Angelus Dómini nuntiávit Maríæ.
℟. Et concépit de Spíritu Sancto.
Ave María...

℣. Ecce ancílla Dómini.
℟. Fiat mihi secúndum verbum tuum.
Ave María...

℣. Et Verbum caro factum est.
℟. Et habitávit in nobis.
Ave María...

℣. Ora pro nobis, Sancta Dei Génitrix.
℟. Ut digni efficiámur promissiónibus Christi.

Orémus.

GRÁTIAM tuam, quæsumus Dómine, méntibus nostris infúnde, ut qui, ángelo nuntiánte, Christi Fílii tui incarnatiónem cognóvimus, per Passiónem ejus et Crucem ad Resurrectiónis glóriam perducámur. Per eúmdem Christum Dóminum nostrum.

℣. The angel of the Lord declared unto Mary.
℟. And she conceived of the Holy Ghost.
Hail Mary...

℣. Behold the handmaid of the Lord.
℟. Be it done unto me according to Thy word.
Hail Mary...

℣. And the Word was made flesh.
℟. And dwelt among us.
Hail Mary...

℣. Pray for us, O holy Mother of God.
℟. That we may be made worthy of the promises of Christ.

Let us pray.

POUR forth, we beseech Thee, O Lord, Thy grace into our hearts, that we to whom the Incarnation of Christ Thy Son was made known by the message of an angel, may, by His Passion and Cross, be brought to the glory of His Resurrection. Through the same Christ our Lord.

Regina Cæli

Regína cæli, lætáre, allelúia.
Quia quem meruísti portáre, allelúia.
Resurréxit sicut dixit, allelúia.
Ora pro nobis Deum, allelúia.

℣. Gaude et lætáre, Virgo María, allelúia.
℟. Quia surréxit Dóminus vere, allelúia.

Orémus.
DEUS, qui per resurrectiónem Fílii tui Dómini nostri Jesu Christi, mundum lætificáre dignátus es, præsta quæsumus ut per ejus Genitrícem Vírginem Maríam perpétuæ capiámus gáudia vitæ. Per eúmdem Christum Dóminum nostrum.

Queen of heaven, rejoice, alleluia.
For He whom thou didst deserve to bear, alleluia.
Hath arisen as He said, alleluia.
Pray for us to God, alleluia.

℣. Rejoice and be glad, O Virgin Mary, alleluia.
℟. For the Lord is truly risen, alleluia.

Let us pray.
O God, Who by the Resurrection of Thy Son, our Lord Jesus Christ, hast vouchsafed to give joy to the whole world; grant, we beseech Thee, that through the intercession of the Virgin Mary, His Mother, we may attain the joys of eternal life. Through the same Christ, our Lord.